WALT DISNEY

WALT
DISNEY
ENTERTAINMENT VISIONARY

by Martin Gitlin

Content Consultant:
M. Thomas Inge, PhD, Blackwell Professor of Humanities
Randolph-Macon College

ABDO
Publishing Company

CREDITS

Published by ABDO Publishing Company, 8000 West 78th Street,
Edina, Minnesota 55439. Copyright © 2010 by Abdo Consulting
Group, Inc. International copyrights reserved in all countries. No
part of this book may be reproduced in any form without written
permission from the publisher. The Essential Library™ is a
trademark and logo of ABDO Publishing Company.

Printed in the United States of America, North Mankato, Minnesota.
012010 102012

Editor: Amy Van Zee
Copy Editor: Paula Lewis
Interior Design and Production: Emily Love
Cover Design: Emily Love

Library of Congress Cataloging-in-Publication Data
Gitlin, Marty.
  Walt Disney : entertainment visionary / by Martin Gitlin.
      p. cm. — (Essential lives)
  Includes bibliographical references and index.
  ISBN 978-1-60453-700-0
  1. Disney, Walt, 1901-1966—Juvenile literature. 2. Animators—
United States—Biography—Juvenile literature. I. Title.

  NC1766.U52 D5417
  791.43092—dc22
  [B]
                                    2008055523

 Manufactured with paper containing
at least 10% post-consumer waste

TABLE OF CONTENTS

Chapter 1   Making of a Mouse   6

Chapter 2   Walt's Wild Imagination   16

Chapter 3   Missed War, New Career   24

Chapter 4   Go West, Young Man   34

Chapter 5   Depressed in the Depression   42

Chapter 6   Seven Dwarfs and One Strike   52

Chapter 7   Television and a Fantasy Land   62

Chapter 8   "M-I-C-K-E-Y M-O-U-S-E!"   70

Chapter 9   Triumph and Tragedy   80

Chapter 10   Honoring a Legend   88

Timeline   96

Essential Facts   100

Additional Resources   102

Glossary   104

Source Notes   106

Index   109

About the Author   112

Mickey Mouse is recognized around the world. This gold figurine was made in Tokyo, Japan.

MAKING OF A MOUSE

Walt Disney had lost his rabbit. Oswald the Lucky Rabbit was not a real rabbit, but Disney's creation.

In 1927, Universal Pictures, which made live-action movies and animated shorts, was eager to start a new cartoon series starring a rabbit. Company founder Carl Laemmle turned to distributor Charles Mintz, who contacted Walt Disney. Animation was in its infancy and Disney was just 25 years old, but Mintz knew talent when he saw it. He believed Disney and his animators were ideal candidates to bring a cartoon rabbit to life.

He was right. Disney and his staff not only drew Oswald, but they took the initiative to create the bunny's first cartoon, titled *Poor Papa*. Universal Pictures was quite satisfied. Oswald the Lucky Rabbit played to enthusiastic crowds. Disney was understandably pleased with the success.

Confident that he would soon be signing a three-year contract with Mintz to continue creating Oswald cartoons, Disney embarked on a vacation with his wife, Lillian, in early February 1928. Everything was going well—but not for long.

Stabbed in the Back

Upon his return, Disney learned that Mintz had sent his brother-in-law, George Winkler, to negotiate with Disney's staff behind his back. The animators had become dissatisfied with what they believed to be low pay and overwork, so they were open to other offers.

A Successful Animator

Friz Freleng was one of the animators of the Oswald cartoons who left Walt Disney to work for Charles Mintz. Freleng eventually became a fixture at Warner Bros. drawing some of the world's most well-known animated figures.

Freleng drew Bugs Bunny, Porky Pig, Tweety Bird, Sylvester the Cat, Yosemite Sam, and other favorites. Freleng also created the animated Pink Panther.

Disney had planned to ask Mintz for an increase from $2,250 to $2,500 for every Oswald cartoon. Mintz informed him that instead, the rate had to be lowered. He also stated that the other animators would quit Disney and take over the job themselves as employees of Mintz's company. Mintz had promised more money to the animators who left Disney and agreed to work directly for Mintz.

Disney was stunned. Universal Pictures owned the copyright to the Oswald character, so he had no leverage to stop the move. He never dreamed his animators would break away. He had known them since they were teenagers. Disney thought of his staff as family and did not think they would turn against him.

His loyal partner, Ub Iwerks, remained with him. The current contract obligated him to produce three more Oswald cartoons, after which his staff was headed to New York, and he and Iwerks were on their own.

Disney felt a deep sense of betrayal, not only from his animators, but also from Mintz and Universal Pictures. Lillian recalled those terrible days when her husband was vowing to never again allow himself to get caught in such a predicament. "He was like a raging lion," Lillian said. "All he could say, over and over, was that he'd never work for anyone again as long as he lived; he'd be his own boss."[1]

Disney immediately threw his energy back into animation. He was determined to create a new character. After brainstorming ideas with Iwerks, the two began to sketch a cartoon about a mouse that built a plane to impress a lady mouse. Disney planned to title the short cartoon *Plane Crazy*. Some say that the mouse character was first named Mortimer. However, that name did not stick. The character was renamed Mickey Mouse.

Plane Crazy

The first Mickey Mouse short cartoon created by Disney was titled *Plane Crazy*. It was inspired by the first solo flight over the Atlantic Ocean. In 1927, Charles Lindbergh piloted the *Spirit of St. Louis* from New York to France. His flight is still considered one of the greatest achievements in aviation history.

A Star Is Born

Disney was not creating Mickey Mouse for Mintz. The contract called only for the continued production of Oswald the Lucky Rabbit, and Disney refused to share his brainstorm with the man he believed had betrayed him. Nor was he going to allow the animators who were leaving Walt Disney Productions to reap any benefits from the creation of Mickey Mouse.

Instead, Disney asked Iwerks to bring Mickey to life. Iwerks drew the animated character in private. He did his best to hide his work, quickly placing drawings of Oswald over those of Mickey whenever anyone entered the room. The animation process was completed in a workshop Disney had constructed in his garage to keep the job top secret.

Disney was anxious to test *Plane Crazy* in front of an audience. He not only convinced a Hollywood theater owner to play it before a feature film, but even persuaded the organist to accompany the cartoon with music. The audience's reaction encouraged

A Famous Voice

Walt Disney provided the high-pitched voice of Mickey Mouse—at least for a while. Disney voiced Mickey from the mouse's creation in 1928 through 1946. He then handed the job to veteran Disney sound and vocal effects man Jim Macdonald, who gave Mickey his voice until 1974. Upon Macdonald's retirement, the task was turned over to veteran voice actor Wayne Allwine, who continues to be the voice of Mickey.

Walt Disney

him to begin work on a second Mickey Mouse cartoon titled *The Gallopin' Gaucho*.

FATEFUL DECISION

By that time, however, Disney was motivated by a personal mission. He decided that Mickey would be the star of one of the earliest animated works with sound. Disney believed both his mouse and his studio would be worldwide sensations if he were successful.

The idea was not revolutionary, but animators had wondered if audiences wanted to hear voices coming from cartoon characters. After all, they were used to hearing other people talk,

Marketing Mickey

Though his work often took him to New York City, Walt Disney generally disliked the city. Raised in rural Missouri, Disney was not attracted to the hustle and bustle of one of the biggest cities in the world.

One of his early excursions to New York occurred in 1928, when he marketed his Mickey Mouse cartoon. This trip reaffirmed his fear of the huge city. Disney had fretted about the trip, partly because he hated being away from home and also because he was uneasy meeting new people. During his visit, he lost his appetite and ten pounds.

That was the least of his problems. Disney was so distraught about being in New York and selling his cartoon that he had difficulty sleeping. He did not fall asleep until at least 2:00 a.m. every night. He even wrote to his brother Roy about his inability to eat or sleep. Adding to his misery, Disney developed a painful sore on his big toe from walking through the streets of New York every day.

• 11 •

"Talkies," such as The Jazz Singer, *changed the entire motion picture industry.*

but quite unaccustomed to listening to animated creatures, particularly one as small and insignificant as a mouse.

Undaunted, Disney forged ahead. Before deciding to give Mickey a voice, he searched for movie studios that would agree to show *Plane Crazy* and *The Gallopin' Gaucho*. The rejections were based on a simple fact: No one had ever heard of Mickey Mouse. Disney, however, was certain that Mickey would be welcomed with open arms if his cartoons featured sound, so he created a third Mickey film titled *Steamboat Willie*.

The task was overwhelming. The technology to produce talking motion pictures, let alone animation with sound, was primitive. How would the sound be timed to match the on-screen action? How would the sound effects be produced? Where would Disney find a sound system to create a recording for the cartoon? Could a studio be found that would purchase the Mickey Mouse creations?

In the summer of 1928, the 26-year-old Disney began searching for answers to those questions. Disney, Iwerks, and fellow animators Wilfred Jackson and Johnny Cannon provided the sound effects, voice, and music for *Steamboat Willie* behind a bed sheet screen. The result was not high in quality, but Disney deemed it effective enough to move forward.

Talking Pictures

Walt Disney's idea to put sound to his animated work was influenced by the first "talkie" live-action movie, *The Jazz Singer*. This Warner Bros. production debuted in theaters in 1927 and marked an end to the silent film era. Disney was among millions of Americans who saw the movie, and his experience proved inspirational. Disney was then determined to bring sound to his Mickey Mouse cartoon.

Disney traveled to New York City, where he met Pat Powers, who ran an independent movie sound system called Cinephone that proved ideal for Disney's needs. The next step was to arrange a recording session to provide music to accompany the cartoon. Powers also made appointments for Disney to show *Steamboat Willie* to distributors, who would take the cartoon to the top movie studios.

All but one distributor, Harry Reichenbach, refused to invest their money into such a radical idea. Reichenbach, who ran the Colony Theater in New York City, gave Disney $1,000 to show *Steamboat Willie* for two weeks. He believed that people would flock in to see one of the first cartoons with sound.

Reichenbach was right. *Steamboat Willie* opened on November 18, 1928, to a full theater. The talking Mickey was an immediate hit. Though he spoke only occasionally in the six-minute cartoon, Mickey soon became one of the most famous characters—animated or otherwise—in the world.

Disney's genius was recognized. But how was that genius first nurtured? How did he develop such a vivid imagination? ⌐

A poster for a 1932 Mickey Mouse cartoon

Flora and Elias Disney around 1937

WALT'S WILD
IMAGINATION

The world might never have known the genius of Walt Disney had it not been for his father's incurable desire to roam. Elias Disney could not stay in one place too long. Kansas,

Colorado, and Missouri were among the states Walt's dad called home. Among his many jobs, he worked as a carpenter and mail carrier. He also tried buying an orange grove in Florida, but after a freeze he lost his crop and sold the grove.

Elias Disney married Flora Call on New Year's Day, 1888. After the birth of their son Herbert in 1888, the couple moved to Chicago, where Elias worked as a home builder. The Disney family continued to grow with the births of Raymond (1890), Roy (1893), Walter Elias (December 5, 1901), and Ruth (1903).

It was not long before Elias felt the need to move on again. He believed Chicago had grown too large and that crime was increasing. He made the decision to move his family to the rural town of Marceline, Missouri, where his brother enjoyed living a peaceful and simple life.

The farm on which the Disney family settled proved to be a perfect place for young Walt to feed his active imagination. He often played in the front yard, which was dotted with weeping willow, cedar, and silver maple trees. The backyard featured an apple orchard that provided a money crop for the family.

Harvest Trouble

One of the most important crops on the Disney farm was apples. The family's ability to pay the bills depended greatly on how many apples they sold.

In 1906, a bountiful apple harvest allowed Elias to purchase 40 additional acres (16 ha) of land. He also offered eldest sons Herbert and Raymond a share of the profits from the 1907 crop if they remained on the farm.

Elias, however, took a big loss on his apples that next year. The huge nationwide apple crop provided much competition and kept prices down. Herbert and Raymond then left the farm, which prompted Elias to sell it.

Walt learned the value of teamwork on the farm. His father and brothers worked with their neighbors to harvest crops such as corn, wheat, and barley, as well as raise cows, chickens, and pigs. The animals were raised for profit and to feed the family. Walt was too young for heavy labor, but he would race into the house to fetch water for the thirsty workers.

Walt also inherited his father's restless nature. As Walt grew older, he often went fishing in a creek in a nearby town. Among the friends he would accompany to his favorite fishing spot was Clem Flickinger, who lived in the farmhouse across the street from him.

"We'd catch catfish and bowheads," Flickinger recalled. "There was a place where the water was four or five feet deep, and me and Walt would take off our clothes and swim. In the winter, a whole bunch of us would go sledding and skating with a big bonfire to keep warm."[1]

Tar Trouble

Sometimes, Walt's curiosity landed him in trouble. One day when his parents were away, he and Ruth began playing with a barrel of tar. The seven-year-old boy claimed that the thick, black, gooey substance could be used as paint. He began to smear the tar on the outside surface of the house. When Ruth, who followed Walt everywhere, asked if the tar could be removed, he insisted it could.

He was, of course, wrong. After he created pictures of houses with smoke coming out of their chimneys with the tar, they discovered to their horror that the tar did not come off. When Elias returned home and saw the mess, he was very angry with Walt. The tar remained on the house for as long as the Disney family lived there.

In the Disney family, Walt became used to beatings—Elias believed strongly in severe punishments for any misbehavior. Roy often comforted him after such lashings. Walt drew closer to his mother, who gently read fairy tales to him to ease his pain and soothe him to sleep.

Model Pig

Walt's favorite animals on the farm were the chickens and pigs. His favorite pig was named Porker, which he recalled to be full of fun and mischief. Walt was so taken by that particular pig that he later used Porker as a model for the Foolish Pig in his animated creation, *The Three Little Pigs.*

Dangerous Ice

One of Walt's bad childhood accidents occurred as he was delivering newspapers. Walt noticed a block of ice on the ground and playfully kicked it. But there was a large nail frozen in the ice, which ended up lodged halfway into his foot. The nail was removed at the hospital, and he was given a tetanus shot. He then had to remain off his feet for two weeks.

One night in 1911, however, the beatings stopped. Elias was in a terrible rage and lifted his hand to strike ten-year-old Walt. By that time, Walt had grown stronger. He grabbed his father's wrist and stared him in the eye. Elias weakened and walked away. He never hit his son again.

Though Walt enjoyed activities such as riding the hogs or competing with Roy at pitching hay, he established an early love for drawing. The lack of paper and pencils in the home forced him to sketch pictures of the farm animals with coal on toilet paper!

RESTLESS STUDENT

Walt had no shortage of confidence, which played a negative role in his class work. He did not understand the importance of learning subjects such as arithmetic. Instead, he sat at his desk and doodled. He even carved his initials into his desk. That same school desk now sits behind a glass case at the school that is named after him.

The Disney family hit hard times after Herbert and Raymond left home. Elias was struck with typhoid fever, a serious disease caused by the contaminated well water on the farm. The family soon sold the farm. They then moved to Kansas City, where Walt took his first job delivering newspapers in the mornings and afternoons.

Walt proved quite ambitious in his mid-teens. At age 16, he began selling newspapers, candy, and soda on the Santa Fe Railroad. He enjoyed that summer as much as any time in his life. The trip on the train took him to Colorado, Oklahoma, and other states, and opened up a new world to him.

Boyhood Hero

Though Walt Disney maintained only average grades, he showed a strong aptitude and keen interest in reading. During his junior high and high school years, he particularly enjoyed reading adventure fiction books about his hero, junior secret agent Jimmy Dale.

Walt's passion for Jimmy Dale helped him forge a friendship with classmate Walter Pfeiffer. They met in 1912, when Disney was 11 years old, and often acted out adventures of the secret agent after school. The two Walts became fast friends. Walt Disney looked forward to visiting his buddy, whose father was kind and generous, unlike his own father. Pfeiffer's father encouraged them in their playacting and even took them to movies on weekends.

It was at those early movies that Walt Disney first saw brilliant silent film star Charlie Chaplin perform. He was so enthralled watching Chaplin's work that he began to favor him in his impressions over Jimmy Dale. Those impressions of Chaplin became strong enough to motivate him to enter amateur talent contests.

Vivid Imagination

Walt did not always follow instructions well in school. On one occasion, the art class teacher asked the students to draw flowers that had been placed in front of them. Instead, Walt drew a series of flowers from his imagination. His flowers featured human hands and faces.

The experience of sleeping in hotels and eating in restaurants by himself gave him a sense of independence.

Walt's love for drawing grew with time. By 1917, his family had returned to Chicago, where his father had invested in the O-Zell Jelly factory. Walt enrolled at William McKinley High School, where he drew editorial cartoons for the school newspaper and eventually became its junior art editor.

Encouraged by his success, he began taking evening classes at the Chicago Institute of Art. He met some of the finest newspaper cartoonists in Chicago. He also met Leroy Gossett, who was well-known for his caricature drawings. The experience motivated Walt's decision to make newspaper cartooning his life's work.

However, in 1914, the War to End All Wars, which later became known as World War I, began. When the United States entered into the war in 1917, Disney's plans—and those of many American men—changed.

After the United States entered World War I, many men were recruited for military duty.

This Red Cross ambulance transported wounded soldiers in France.

MISSED WAR, NEW CAREER

sense of patriotism and adventure overcame Walt Disney in 1918. That was not unusual. Similar feelings washed over many young Americans when the United States entered World War I. Among them were brothers Roy and

Raymond; both young men were serving in the U.S. armed forces and planned to fight.

After finishing high school, Walt visited Roy, who was training at the Great Lakes Naval Station. That trip strengthened Walt's desire to join the military. There was just one problem. Because he was only 16 years old, parental permission was required to enlist.

Elias and Flora were not about to let a third son go off to battle. However, Walt would not take no for an answer. He was able to convince his mother to sign a document allowing him to become a volunteer for the International Red Cross. Although he was only 16, he changed a digit in his birth year to meet the age requirement of 17. He was sent to Chicago to learn how to drive an ambulance. He was then sent to Connecticut. While there, the armistice that ended World War I was signed.

Nevertheless, Walt was shipped to France. He remained in France for about one year. Boredom set in quickly. There was simply little for Walt to do aside from driving military personnel around France and Germany.

That gave Walt plenty of time to create new ideas, including one that proved quite profitable. He and a friend nicknamed Cracker bought surplus

German helmets and shot holes in them to make them appear as if they had been used in combat. Walt used his artistic talent to paint German insignias on the helmets for added authenticity and sold them as souvenirs to U.S. soldiers who were about to return home. The scheme earned him $300—more money than he had ever seen.

To Go or Not to Go

Walt Disney certainly yearned to join his brothers overseas during World War I, but his yearning to return home was often just as great after he arrived in France. He wrote to the *McKinley Voice*, his high school newspaper, that "France is an interesting place, but just the same I want to . . ." and he inserted a cartoon of a man shouting "OH! I want to go home to my Mama."[1]

By that time, brothers Roy and Herbert had already returned to the United States. Walt, however, could not decide whether he wanted to follow them back. He considered reenlisting and transferring to Albania, where Red Cross workers were earning $150 a month—nearly triple his salary in France. On August 7, 1919, Disney finally made up his mind and put in for a discharge. After several delays, the ship that transported him from France docked in New York. Disney had spent nearly a year in Europe, during which time he had saved almost $600.

HEADING HOME

Soon Walt was joining other men on a steamship back to New York. He quickly left the city and met his parents back in Chicago. Elias proudly announced that he had set up Walt with a job in what was now the family jelly business, but he was stunned when his son declined the offer. Walt told his father he would return to Kansas City to pursue a career as an artist.

The next morning, Walt was on his way to the city of his past to map out his future. He moved into the old family home with Roy and Herbert and immediately applied for a job as a cartoonist with the *Kansas City Star*, the largest newspaper in town. He was turned down on the spot—the editors never even bothered to look at his drawings. The rejection sent Walt into a deep depression.

Roy informed him of an opening for artists at the Pesmen-Rubin Studios, a new advertising agency. Walt showed them his sketches and drawings and was thrilled to be hired immediately. He was officially a professional artist.

The job was far from glamorous. Walt drew advertisements and letterheads featuring tractors or hens laying eggs for companies dealing in agriculture. But he did not draw

The Joker

During his youth and his teenage years, Walt loved pulling practical jokes. On one occasion, he dressed up like a woman, knocked on the front door of his home, and began to pepper his mother with silly questions.

Flora had no idea the "stranger" was her son. The disguise was truly convincing—he had even put on a wig and makeup. She only became wise to the gag when she realized that the "woman" was wearing one of her dresses.

Although he worked hard, Walt Disney did not always find success as a cartoonist.

them for long. Pesmen-Rubin terminated Walt's position after one month.

Working with Iwerks

The experience, however, did bring one benefit. At Pesmen-Rubin, Walt forged a friendship with Ub Iwerks, who had been hired and laid off at the same time. Walt, now more depressed than ever about his future, was working at the post office. One day, Ub knocked on the door of Walt's home. Walt and Ub sat in the kitchen and talked past midnight. They decided that if no one wanted them as artists, they should start a business of their own. Iwerks-Disney Commercial Artists was born.

What they needed was business. Disney's old friend Walt Pfeiffer pointed them in the right direction. Pfeiffer's father was a member of the Leatherworkers Union, which quickly hired Iwerks-Disney to design their newsletter. That earned them $135, but despite their efforts, it was their only assignment. No other company wanted to hire a couple of kids who had yet to celebrate their twentieth birthdays.

Iwerks soon displayed his unselfishness. In January 1920, he showed Disney a help-wanted ad for

The Eye Business?

Walt Disney and Ub Iwerks had originally titled their new business venture Disney-Iwerks Commercial Artists before deciding to transpose their last names.

Why did they switch the last names around? Because after seeing the title Disney-Iwerks listed in the lobby of the Railroad Exchange Building, they felt that it sounded like an eyeglass company.

a cartoonist for the Kansas City Slide Company, which was later renamed the Kansas City Film Ad Company. Rather than apply for the job himself, he encouraged his buddy to do so. Disney was hired, but he did not forget his best friend.

The work allowed Disney to get in on the ground floor of the animated film industry. Felix the Cat had become the first popular cartoon character in 1919. The earliest cartoon characters had gained popularity because they moved like the silent movie comedians of the day, such as Charlie Chaplin, Harold Lloyd, and Buster Keaton.

Soon the demand grew for animation in advertising. The Kansas City Film Ad Company used crude stick figures, which Disney drew. The one-minute commercials were a hit with movie audiences simply because they were animated. Soon the company needed more cartoonists,

Drawings That Move

Disney dreamed for several years of working as a newspaper cartoonist. But when he was given the opportunity to work as a cartoonist at the *Kansas City Star*, he rejected it.

By that time, he had gained employment at the Kansas City Film Ad Company and had immersed himself in learning about animation. Making cartoon figures move proved far more thrilling to him than drawing lifeless ones.

and Disney quickly recommended Iwerks, who was hired. The team was back together.

Both had much to learn. Disney could draw, but had yet to be taught how to work a camera or master any other aspect of developing animation. He studied the process and searched for ways to improve the process and technology. He borrowed a camera from the company and began working in a crude studio he built in his family's garage. He experimented with lighting and camera angles.

Disney was fascinated by animation. He soon realized that the movement of cartoon characters could be used to express emotion. He threw himself into his work. He completed one-minute cartoons with story lines that local movie patrons would appreciate and sold them to the Newman Theater as "Newman Laugh-O-Grams." He returned home from work at the Kansas City

Hidden Camera

Ub Iwerks was shy with women, so Disney decided to take advantage of it. Iwerks was attracted to a woman named Margaret Metzinger at the Kansas City Film Ad Company, but could not summon the courage to ask her out. So Disney invited both Iwerks and Metzinger to the same restaurant. As Iwerks and his date became acquainted, Disney secretly recorded it with his film camera.

When Iwerks arrived at work the next day, Disney was showing the film of the entire date to their coworkers. The joke backfired. The embarrassed Iwerks walked out of the room and Metzinger threw a bottle of ink at Disney.

Film Ad Company every day to create new Laugh-O-Grams. His career was taking off. But his home life was on the verge of collapse. ⌒

Charlie Chaplin, a silent film star known for his physical comedy,
was an inspiration for cartoon humor.

Hollywood, California, pictured in 1925

Go West, Young Man

The future seemed bright for young Walt Disney in Kansas City. He had coupled his Laugh-O-Grams cartoons with his work at the Film Ad Company to create a promising career. But soon that bright future faded.

Signs of trouble appeared in the Disney family. Elias lost all the money he invested when the jelly factory failed. Walt's parents and his sister Ruth were forced to move into the Kansas City home Walt was sharing with his brothers and Herbert's wife.

Then, Herbert landed a job in Portland, Oregon. Roy was stricken with tuberculosis—a lung disease that was common during that era. Elias and Flora decided to accompany Ruth to Oregon to live with Herbert and his wife.

Walt was now alone. His Laugh-O-Grams business had become successful enough to motivate him to bring in several young animators. He promised great experience and an opportunity to become noticed. When a group of Kansas City businessmen agreed to invest $15,000 in the Laugh-O-Grams, the sky appeared to be the limit for the 20-year-old cartoonist.

Encouraged by his success, Disney quit the Film Ad Company. He lured Iwerks to do the same and join him in the Laugh-O-Grams business. The animators churned out cartoons of well-known fairy tales such as *Little Red Riding Hood*, *Jack and the Beanstalk*, and *Cinderella*. Disney even used the knowledge gained from studying cartooning to combine animation with the photography of a live actress and create a short film titled *Alice's Wonderland*.

Ultimately, however, he had underestimated the amount of money required to run a business and survive on his own. Iwerks returned to the Kansas City Film Ad Company in 1922, and Disney's Laugh-O-Grams business went bankrupt the following year. Disney believed, however, that his experience could land him in the movie business. So he boarded a train and headed to the film capital of the world: Hollywood, California.

Horrible Start in Hollywood

The silent movie industry was booming when Disney arrived in California, but major studios such as MGM and Warner Bros. had yet to take hold. Disney believed he could become a movie director.

He moved into the Los Angeles home of his uncle Robert, and then set off to search for directing jobs.

Ub's Family Life

Ub Iwerks was born Ubbe Iwwerks, but he shortened his name before he went into business with Disney. Ub Iwerks had a difficult childhood in Kansas City. His father Evert, a Dutch immigrant, abandoned the family when Ub was in high school, which forced Ub to give up his education and get a job. Iwerks never forgave his father. When Evert died and Ub was asked what he wanted done with the body, he reportedly replied, "Throw it in a ditch."[1] Ub refused to talk about his father during interviews.

He received a rude awakening in the form of rejection after rejection. He found that he was simply too young and inexperienced. Disney had exhausted all his options in one week, after which he had just five dollars to his name. During a trip to the hospital to visit Roy, who was still recuperating from the bout of tuberculosis, Walt broke down and cried. Roy suggested that his brother return to animation despite the fact that the industry was thriving in New York City. Walt took Roy's advice and began doing the same work he had produced in Kansas City. Only this time, he used a Hollywood flavor.

Although one local theater chain purchased his new cartoons, he found little success. However, he contacted Margaret Winkler, a distributor who had expressed an interest in *Alice's Wonderland* before Disney had left Kansas City. He sent a sample to Winkler and began working on a

Walt the Actor

The only job Disney found as he sought work as a movie director in Hollywood was as an extra actor in a silent film. Disney was hired to wear a cavalry uniform and ride a horse. But it rained the day his scene was to be shot, and the filming was cancelled. When filming began again, a new group of riders had been hired and Disney was not among them. His acting career was over before it really began.

series of *Alice* cartoons. Winkler loved his work. She agreed to distribute each of Disney's *Alice's Wonderland* shorts for $1,500 apiece. On the verge of going broke, Disney finally got a break.

An Upturn

Grateful for Roy's suggestion, Disney returned to the hospital to visit his brother. Roy asked if Walt could continue producing *Alice* films for $1,500. Walt explained that he could make each film for $750 and still make a $750 profit. Walt then added, "I can't possibly do it unless you come in with me. I need your help, Roy. You've just got to get out of here and join me. Please say you'll do it."[2]

Rock Bottom

In the fall of 1922, Walt Disney was broke. His landlady kicked him out for failure to pay his rent. Forced to move into his office, Disney slept on sheets of canvas that he had placed on the floor near the drawing board.

Disney could not even afford to eat. He ran up a $60 bill at the local restaurant. One of the owners told him they could not give him any more meals until he paid his bill.

The most humiliating incident occurred in December 1922. A dentist named Thomas B. McCrum offered to pay Disney $500 to create a short film teaching children the benefits of brushing their teeth. McCrum asked Disney to come to his office to sign the deal. Disney replied that he could not meet McCrum that night. The reason? Disney's only pair of shoes was being repaired, and he did not have the money to pay the bill. McCrum offered to pay the shoemaker.

His brother did not jump at the opportunity, but he gave it careful thought. Roy checked out of the hospital the next day despite the doctors' concern whether he had fully recovered from his illness. Soon Roy was emptying his bank account and sinking all his money into the newly formed studio.

While Roy handled the business end, Walt did the cartooning and writing for the *Alice* cartoons. Though Winkler began complaining about what she perceived as low-quality animation, she ordered 12 more. Walt was a talented artist and storyteller, but it soon became apparent that he lacked the animation skills of the best in the business.

Walt was not too proud to admit his shortcomings, so he summoned Iwerks to join him in Hollywood. The loyal friend joined Disney Brothers Studio in 1924. The quality of animation in the *Alice* cartoons improved under Iwerks's guidance.

Another momentous event in Walt's life occurred in early 1925.

Job Offer

It was not easy for Disney to lure Ub Iwerks from Kansas City to Hollywood. Iwerks had received a raise from the Kansas City Film Ad Company and was making $50 a week when Disney called with an offer of just $20 a week. Disney had to increase the offer as well as give Iwerks part ownership in the new company. Only then did Iwerks join him in Hollywood.

Wedding Bells

Walt's brother Roy also got married in 1925. He married his longtime sweetheart. Roy had known Edna Frances since childhood, but his illness had prevented him from asking her to marry him. When he was finally well, he sent for Edna and they were married. They had been engaged four years.

Lillian Bounds was hired as an inker at the studio, and he became smitten with the young woman. The romance blossomed quickly and on July 13, 1925, Walt and Lillian were married in Lewiston, Idaho.

Walt had found fulfillment in both his personal and professional lives. After he created a mouse named Mickey, he would become one of the most famous people in America.

A poster advertising one of the Alice comedies

The Great Depression left many people in the United States homeless and unemployed.

DEPRESSED IN THE
DEPRESSION

In 1926, Walt Disney decided to change the company name from Disney Brothers Studio to Walt Disney Studio. Some sources say that Roy suggested the name change, and other sources

called the new studio Walt Disney Productions.
In the 1980s, many portions of the company were
joined under the name Walt Disney Company, which
is what it is known as today.

But in 1926, Disney encountered another
setback. Early that year, Disney was informed that
Margaret Winkler had turned over control of her
distribution business to her new husband, Charles
Mintz. Mintz came to Disney with bad news—the
contract to continue creating the *Alice* cartoons was
being cancelled due to lack of interest.

The news devastated Disney. He locked himself
into his office and spoke to no one for days while
blaming himself for the failure of his studio. But
as he lamented his fate, Mintz was working on a
deal with Universal Pictures founder Carl Laemmle
that would allow Disney to create a cartoon rabbit
to compete with the immensely popular *Felix the Cat*
animated series.

Laemmle held a rather low opinion of Disney
animation at the time, but Mintz convinced him
to give the studio a chance. The animators worked
tirelessly on sketching the black rabbit. Much to his
surprise, Laemmle liked what Mintz named Oswald
the Lucky Rabbit enough to give Disney the job.

The Oswald cartoons hit the theaters early in 1927, but were eventually taken away by Mintz, Universal Pictures, and Disney's animators. That led to the creation of Mickey Mouse.

Disney hired new animators as the popularity of Mickey and girlfriend Minnie Mouse grew. By the end of 1929, as the beginning of the Great Depression signaled one of the worst financial periods in U.S. history, Mickey had grown into the biggest name in animation. But Disney understood that he needed to expand his stable of characters to ensure future success.

Begging and Pleading

During the late 1920s, Disney worked hard to recruit some of the top animators in the country. Among those whom Disney attempted to lure to his studio included Otto Messmer and Al Eugster, the primary animators of the highly popular Felix the Cat. "It was pressure!" remembered Messmer. "(Disney) begged and pleaded."[1] The two animators, however, opted to remain in New York and continue drawing Felix.

A "SILLY" IDEA

Disney's first move was the creation of a new cartoon series titled *Silly Symphonies*. Each episode featured different characters and themes. This gave Disney and his animators an opportunity to test out new animated characters. Disney sold the first *Silly Symphony*, which was called *The Skeleton Dance*, to a Hollywood theater. It received rave reviews from the critics. But not all was rosy. As the Depression worsened, few Americans could afford to attend movies. That, combined with the cost of animation, caused hardship for Walt Disney Studio.

Though Mickey Mouse remained popular, the company was spiraling downward again toward financial ruin. One contributing factor for the financial failure was the contract Disney had signed with distributor Pat Powers. He was paying Powers $26,000 for the use of his Cinephone sound equipment. When Disney traveled to New York to meet with Powers in January 1930, he was met with unexpected news. First, Powers offered Disney an incredible $130,000 a year to give up his studio and go to work for him.

Disney, however, had worked so hard to create his own studio that he was not about to give it up. When he turned down the offer, Powers informed him that he had offered the invaluable Iwerks three times more money than Disney was making to start his own animation studio.

When Disney called his friend, Iwerks confirmed that he was indeed leaving to open his own business. Disney was stunned. Not only was his friend and best animator leaving, but so was musical director Carl Stallings. Disney was forced to break ties with Powers, whom he still owed $150,000. Disney could not sell his cartoons to other distributors because Powers still owned the rights to them. He also had to return the sound equipment to Powers.

The desperate Disney brothers found an ally in Harry Cohn, the president of Columbia Pictures. Cohn threatened to sue Powers if he attempted to prevent them from selling their cartoons. Powers backed off and sold his contract to the Disney brothers for $50,000. But the loss of Iwerks and Stallings was still quite painful.

Disney managed to save his studio, but the process took a terrible personal toll on him. Lillian's inability to become pregnant led to further emotional distress. She and Walt had been trying to have a baby since their wedding, but without success. A doctor had assured Lillian she was not to blame, which led Walt to fear there was something physically wrong with him.

Jealousy

Most men are thrilled when their brothers become fathers, but Walt was not one of them. In January 1930, Walt became jealous over the birth of Roy's first son, Roy Edward. Walt could not feel joy for his brother and sister-in-law because he and Lillian had failed to have a child of their own.

Walt and Lillian Disney in Hawaii in 1934

Getting Away from It All

Disney, who was just 29 years old, soon lost his appetite and fell into a deep depression. He was silent around family and friends. He often locked himself in his studio and just stared out the window.

"I guess I was working too hard and worrying too much," Disney later explained.

I had a nervous breakdown. . . . Costs were going up; each new picture we finished cost more to make than we had figured it would earn when we first began to plan it. . . . I cracked up. [2]

Soon the doctor was recommending that Disney be hospitalized. Lillian rejected that idea, which led the doctor to offer his opinion that the only alternative was a long vacation that would allow her husband to get away from work and relax. She and Walt traveled to several cities in the United States before boarding a ship to Cuba, where they remained for a week. After a stop in Panama, they

---

Fore!

The doctor did not simply prescribe rest and relaxation to help Disney emerge from his depression in 1930. He also told Disney to get plenty of exercise. Disney tried several activities, but some of them made him more frustrated. He attempted wrestling and boxing before taking up golf. But it did not help him relax—he would become quite angry when he missed a shot.

Disney then took up horseback riding, which led to polo, a sport that is played while riding a horse. He had finally found an activity he enjoyed. Disney became quite a good polo player. Disney was so taken with polo that he tried to convince many of his coworkers to learn the sport as well. After several years honing his skills, he joined the Riviera Club, which counted as members such celebrities as movie star Spencer Tracy and comedian and actor Will Rogers.

returned to Hollywood, where Disney jumped right back into his work.

The trip lasted two months and revitalized Disney. One of the first producers to create successful animated talkies now planned on making color cartoons. Roy had signed a contract with United Artists, but was skeptical about that company giving Walt Disney Studio money for color animation. Disney, however, believed the public would want to see cartoons in color, so he began planning dozens of *Silly Symphonies* in color.

Disney's first foray into color cartooning was titled *Flowers and Trees,* which debuted in July 1932. Meanwhile, the success of Mickey and the *Silly Symphonies* motivated Disney to increase his staff of animators. He also agreed to have teachers from the Chouinard Art Institute in Los Angeles teach classes at his studio.

Disney was soon recognized for his work. He won Academy Awards that November for the creation of Mickey Mouse and for *Flowers and Trees.* He was widely acclaimed the next year for his *Silly Symphony* creation titled *The Three Little Pigs.* Movie enthusiasts crowded the theaters to watch the pigs outwit the Big Bad Wolf.

A Generous Man

The addition of first daughter Diane Marie to the Disney family six days before Christmas in 1933 apparently had quite an effect on her father. To celebrate the occasion, Disney declared that from that point forward, all orphans would receive free admission to any theater on the first day his new pictures were showing.

While Walt basked in the glow of success, Lillian gave birth to Diane Marie, their first child. The man who had been deeply depressed just two years earlier was now rich, famous, and happy. ⌁

In the 1930s, Walt Disney's animation was becoming increasingly popular.

Walt Disney received an Honorary Master of Arts degree from Harvard University in 1938.

SEVEN DWARFS AND ONE STRIKE

aughter Diane was not the only addition to Walt Disney's life as the mid-1930s approached. Donald, Pluto, and Goofy were among the new animated characters created by the Disney studio, which housed 200 employees by the end of 1934.

Disney also began marketing his creations. Three Little Pigs and Big Bad Wolf dolls were sold to coincide with the release of his animated film, *The Three Little Pigs*. The dolls brought in several hundred thousand dollars, which meant that Disney turned an annual profit for the first time. *The Three Little Pigs* was immensely popular. By the end of 1933, it had earned $125,000, far more than any previous cartoon short in history. As 1934 came to a close, the total had skyrocketed to $250,000.

But as the Depression worsened, a drop in theater attendance forced owners to take drastic measures. They lowered prices, offered double features, and held raffles to attract business. Many also eliminated cartoon shorts because they could no longer afford them. Disney wasted no time in responding to the problem.

A Rally Cry

The question "Who's Afraid of the Big Bad Wolf?" that was sung repeatedly by all three pigs in Disney's *The Three Little Pigs* cartoon took on added meaning during the Depression. The refrain became a rallying cry for Americans to fight fear in the face of economic disaster. Many believed the line inspired U.S. President Franklin Roosevelt to utter his famous Depression-era plea to the American people, "The only thing we have to fear is fear itself."[1]

In late 1934, he decided to make the first full-length animated film.

SEVEN DWARFS, SEVEN DAYS A WEEK

Disney decided to make an animated version of the fairy tale *Snow White and the Seven Dwarfs*. The task of creating such a film was enormous. Every department at the studio would be required to work overtime to meet Disney's goal of completing the project in three years. And everyone had a role.

The music department wrote and rejected 25 songs before settling on the ones that made the cut. The story writers and animators worked tirelessly to create characters such as Snow White, the seven dwarfs (named Bashful, Doc, Dopey, Grumpy, Happy, Sleepy, and Sneezy), and the Wicked Queen that would appeal to movie audiences. Every animator was responsible for specific scenes.

Funny Animals

Among the most accomplished young animators of the 1920s and 1930s was Walter Lantz, who would gain increasing fame. The Walter Lantz Studio became best known in the 1940s for its creation of Woody Woodpecker, a mischievous bird that featured a similar personality to that of the equally famous Daffy Duck. The reason? Woody and Daffy were both originally conceived by animator Ben Hardaway.

Adriana Caselotti provided the voice of the animated Snow White.

Meanwhile, the staff scoured the country to find appropriate voices for everything from the Magic Mirror to the whistling birds.

Many outside and inside the studio believed Disney had gone too far. The time and expense of creating a full-length animated movie was overwhelming and most thought that it would not hold the attention of movie audiences. The project became widely known as "Disney's Folly." Disney also planned to tinker with the plot. Because Snow White and the Wicked Queen were considered to be the least interesting characters in the film, the roles of the Seven Dwarfs were increased based on the assumption that they brought more humor to the story.

The production required all of Disney's energies. Even after he and Lillian adopted a second daughter, two-week-old Sharon Mae, on New Year's Day 1936, he devoted himself to the studio.

Producing the film put the Disney studio deeply in debt. But the money would be made back—and then some. *Snow White and the Seven Dwarfs* premiered at the Carthay Circle Theater in Hollywood four days before Christmas in 1937. And though the Depression was at its height at the time, 20 million patrons attended their local movie houses to see it. They watched spellbound as a fantasy world played out before their eyes.

Critics were equally impressed. One from the *New York Herald Tribune* wrote, "After seeing *Snow White* for the third time, I am more certain than ever that it belongs with the few great masterpieces of the screen."[2] *Time* magazine even put Disney's picture on its cover. The film earned more than $8 million, twice as much as any previous film in history. At the 1938 Academy Awards, Disney was presented with a Special Award Oscar for himself and seven little trophies, one for each dwarf.

A Tragic End

In the midst of success came tragedy. In November 1938, Disney's parents experienced a gas furnace accident in their home near Los Angeles. His mother, Flora, died from inhaling the fumes.

Directorial Debut

Not everything Disney touched turned to gold. *The Golden Touch*, which directly followed the highly successful *The Three Little Pigs*, was a failure. *The Golden Touch* was a *Silly Symphony* based on the fairy tale about King Midas in which everything the king touched turned instantly to gold. King Midas became very greedy upon discovering his talent until he learned that he could not "touch" people—that is, interact or be friends with them.

Disney directed and controlled every aspect of the production of *The Golden Touch*. In Disney's version, the story concluded with the king realizing he was just another person and showing it by going out to buy a hamburger. Though none of Disney's employees expressed their disappointment at his directorial debut to his face, the film was criticized. It also fared poorly at the box office. Disney was upset when he realized that his short film had failed. He quickly removed *The Golden Touch* from distribution and never again directed an animated or live-action film.

His father survived, but was never the same mentally or emotionally.

Disney had become one of the most famous people in the United States. The success of *Snow White and the Seven Dwarfs* brought more attention to his *Mickey Mouse* and *Silly Symphony* shorts. Disney, however, discontinued *Silly Symphonies* in 1939 to concentrate on more full-length animated films—*Pinocchio*, *Fantasia*, and *Bambi*.

STRIKE AT THE STUDIO

As war clouds gathered over Europe in the late 1930s, much of the foreign market for films declined, as did the attention of American movie patrons. Though *Pinocchio* and *Fantasia* were well received and praised by critics, the earnings from ticket sales failed to match the production costs for the movies. And as work began on *Bambi*, dark clouds also gathered over the Disney studio.

Family

Disney felt great pain over the gas accident that took his mother's life in the home that he had bought for his parents. It also deeply affected Disney's father, Elias, in his last years. Years later, Disney's daughter Sharon asked her father at which cemetery his parents were buried. Sharon dropped the subject when she noticed tears welling up in Disney's eyes.

Many of the 1,500 employees believed they were overworked and underpaid. In May 1941, they formed a union and went on strike. Disney refused to give in to any demands in the belief that the strike would last only a few days. Not only did it continue, but it also grew violent. Strikers set up a picket line to prevent any employees from entering the building. They taunted Disney as he arrived for work. Disney, who valued loyalty above everything else, was hurt by what he believed to be the betrayal of his staff.

During the strike, the U.S. State Department asked Disney to travel to South America on a goodwill tour. While he was gone, his brother Roy settled the strike by recognizing the new Cartoonist Guild union. But Disney's relationship with his animators would never be the same.

On December 7, 1941, Japanese planes bombed the U.S. naval base

Studio Woes

Disney's success in the late 1930s allowed him to build a new studio in Burbank, California, at a cost of $3 million. The new studio contributed, however, to the dissatisfaction of many of his employees. They wondered why he spent that much money on a new studio rather than on increasing their salaries. It also played a role in the employees going on strike a few years later.

at Pearl Harbor in Hawaii. The following day, the United States officially entered World War II. The role of the Disney studio in U.S. society was about to be drastically altered. ⌐

Mickey Mouse's face decorated this fighter pilot's plane.

Disney, second from left, sketched a model of a Mickey Mouse gas mask for children to use for protection during World War II.

TELEVISION AND A FANTASY LAND

Disney received a call from the U.S. Army on December 7, 1941, just hours after the Japanese bombed Pearl Harbor. He was informed that hundreds of soldiers were about to be transported to the studio. The size of the studio made it an ideal antiaircraft base, which was needed in case the Japanese expanded their bombing to California and the nearby Lockheed aircraft plant.

The military also required Disney to aid the war effort in another way. He was to produce a series of training films, including shorts on aircraft identification. The army occupied the studio for eight months, after which the threat of Japanese invasion was deemed over. But Disney continued making war-training films for little money, which left him with little time for commercial ventures.

The Depression and World War II proved financially devastating to the Disney studio. The company owed more than $4 million to the Bank of America, which prevented Disney from creating the expensive animated films that he had planned, such as *Peter Pan* and *Alice in Wonderland*.

Disney then went in a different direction. Soon he was producing his first live-action movies, though *Song of the South* included some animation. But *Song of the South* and *So Dear to My Heart*, a musical about a pioneer family, failed to relieve the financial hardship.

Daddy

Sharon stated that while growing up, she and Diane were not aware that their father was famous. "We weren't raised with the idea that this was a great man," she said. "He was Daddy."[1]

What did prove popular following the war, however, was a series of nature films titled *True-Life Adventures*. These films not only allowed the studio to chip away at its debts, but also gave Disney and his brother Roy the freedom to produce *Peter Pan*, *Alice in Wonderland*, and *Cinderella*, as well as *Treasure Island*, their first highly successful live-action film.

Due to its similarity to *Snow White and the Seven Dwarfs*, Disney believed *Cinderella* would make a greater splash than the others. And he was right. It proved nearly as popular as *Snow White* upon its release in March 1950. Theaters were also packed for showings of *Treasure Island* that same year. *Alice in Wonderland* did not fare as well, but *Peter Pan* was a hit in 1953.

Wedding Day

Disney's busy work schedule screeched to a halt on May 9, 1954. His older daughter, Diane, was getting married that day. Diane married football player Ron Miller, who played for the University of Southern California and later in the National Football League as a receiver for the Los Angeles Rams.

TURNING TO TELEVISION

By that time, however, fewer people were looking to the big screen for entertainment. Television had become all the rage in America, and Disney looked to cash in on its popularity. He struck a deal with ABC—the smallest of the three existing networks—to produce a weekly television program.

The contract called for ABC to pay Disney $500,000. But that was a small sum compared to the $4.5 million the network would loan Disney for his dream project. That dream project was called Disneyland. The television show was titled *Disneyland* to get children and their families excited about the theme park Disney was planning. The show debuted on October 27, 1954. The deal also gave ABC one-third ownership in the park.

The show was filmed in color despite the fact that it would be aired in black and white. Disney recognized that someday all

Home Choo Choo

Walt Disney enjoyed very little free time, but he did start a hobby in 1949 that proved quite ambitious. He and Lillian bought a new home that year. Disney spent hundreds of hours building a half-mile of train tracks that circled their home. Trains had been of great interest to Disney since he worked selling items such as newspapers, candy, and soda on the Santa Fe Railroad as a teenager.

The train tracks Disney constructed around his house were far from miniature. They were built for scale-model trains that were large enough for adults to sit in. He and his studio coworkers built a steam-driven train engine that was strong enough to pull Disney and several visitors. It even featured a winding tunnel that ran 120 feet (37 m). The tunnel was so long and dark that riders could not see the end of the tunnel as they began going through it.

The trains provided Disney welcome relaxation and relief from the pressures of running a studio. So did other novelties in his home, which included a movie theater and soda fountain. This marked the first period of Disney's professional life in which he was able to take his mind off work through hobbies he could enjoy at home.

Television sets became popular in U.S. homes in the 1950s.

television programs would be shown in color. The program featured a mixture of fantasy, adventure, and education. Disney served as the master of ceremonies for the show. He had become famous for his work behind the scenes. Now he would become more famous for his work in front of the camera. His show was an immediate hit. An estimated 75 million people watched television that evening—31 million of those viewers watched the first episode of *Disneyland*.

Disneyland was soon the only ABC program rated among the top 15 on television. The stories on the *Disneyland* show included "Davy Crockett—King of the Wild Frontier," which was so popular in the late 1950s that it seemed as if every young boy in America was wearing a Davy Crockett coonskin cap.

The undertaking of producing a television show, however, paled in comparison to opening and maintaining a theme park. Roy was opposed to the project and let his brother know it in no uncertain terms. He even threatened that he would provide no money for Disneyland.

"We're in the motion picture business," Roy told Disney. "We're in the animated-film business. We don't know anything about this entertainment business. I don't look at that as a very good omen."[2]

WORKING OUT THE KINKS

When Disneyland opened on July 17, 1955, the $17 million park was flooded with invited guests. Disney was required to open the park

Guests at Home

A polite and courteous staff at Disneyland was very important to the man who created it. On one occasion, Disney and Lillian were about to enter an exhibit, but the guard at the entrance would not let them through. When Disney identified himself, the guard allowed him to pass, but refused entrance to Lillian, whom the guard did not know was his wife. Disney fired the guard on the spot. He then called the staff together and explained to them that all guests at Disneyland must be treated as if they were guests at his own home.

Cleanliness

Disney was obsessed with keeping his theme park sparkling clean. That priority was formed on a trip to Europe, during which time he visited several amusement parks. Disney found most of them to be dirty and unappealing, but he was quite impressed with one in Denmark called Tivoli Gardens that was immaculate and affordable.

because ABC had set aside that day to show the festivities on national television. But Disneyland simply was not ready. There were not enough rides, which resulted in long lines for those that were available. Some rides broke down. Folks complained on the sultry day that there were not enough drinking fountains. The asphalt on one street had not yet set, causing women's high-heeled shoes to become stuck in the pavement. Many visitors complained as they left the park.

The opening day problems were just a temporary setback. Soon the rides were fixed and the workers sent the visitors through the lines with greater speed. Seven weeks after its opening, Disneyland had welcomed 1 million visitors from across the country and even other parts of the world.

Just when folks began to think Walt Disney could not get any larger, another television program hit the airwaves on October 3, 1955. And it seemed not a child in the United States would even think about missing it.

Many believe that the Neuschwanstein Castle in Germany was Disney's inspiration for Cinderella's Castle at Disneyland.

Prop men work on the set of 20,000 Leagues Under the Sea.

"M-I-C-K-E-Y M-O-U-S-E!"

While the planning and opening of the new theme park occupied most of Disney's time in the mid-1950s, his movie ventures continued with great success. He based a live-action movie on the Jules Verne classic book, *20,000 Leagues Under the Sea.* This film featured movie stars Kirk Douglas, Peter Lorre, and British actor James Mason. Disney animation did not take a backseat, as folks jammed into the theaters to see *Lady and the Tramp* as well.

Soon, however, Disney would launch what would blossom into one of the most famous programs in the history of television. Just three months after the opening of Disneyland, *The Mickey Mouse Club* debuted. It featured Disney cartoons and educational shorts, as well as a group of children called Mouseketeers.

Many young children in the United States watched the show faithfully every weekday and admired popular Mouseketeers such as Annette and Cubby. Those same young viewers would sing *The Mickey Mouse Club* theme song right along with the Mouseketeers on television: "Who's the leader of the club that's made for you and me? M-I-C-K-E-Y M-O-U-S-E."[1]

The Mickey Mouse Club hit the airwaves less than one year after the debut of the *Disneyland* program, but it did not detract from the popularity of that show. The "Davy Crockett" episodes remained the most watched program on television. *Zorro*, a show about a swashbuckling swordsman, debuted in 1957 and added to the Disney television empire.

DISNEY, DISNEY, EVERYWHERE

The soaring ratings that made advertisers happy were not the only source of income for Disney. His products were everywhere. Disney characters were made into dolls and other toys. And suddenly the most popular watch in the country featured the huge smile of Mickey Mouse.

Disney had reached the pinnacle of his

Big Circus, Small Loss

Although Disneyland brought in $11 million in six months in 1955 and $24.5 million in 1956, Walt Disney was concerned. He fretted that not enough people would be visiting the park during the Christmas holidays.

He had what he thought was a solution. He created the Mickey Mouse Club Circus, which would run from late November through New Year's Day. Disney had always dreamed of running a circus, and his idea would give him the opportunity. Unfortunately, Disney's fears turned into reality even with the new venture. Attendance proved quite disappointing at the Mickey Mouse Club Circus, which led him to conclude that with so much to do at Disneyland, visitors to the park simply did not want to spend two hours in one spot.

He also realized too late that a circus was not unique—folks could attend them just about anywhere. Since most people had been to one or more circuses in their lifetimes, they did not want to spend time on a trip to Disneyland attending an activity they had already experienced. The circus experiment cost Disney $125,000, but that was not much compared to the huge amount of money Disneyland was bringing in.

career. There seemed little more he could accomplish. In the late 1950s, Disney began to spend more time with his growing extended family, which now included three grandchildren. Soon his second daughter, Sharon, would tie the knot with an architect named Bob Brown. Disney was unhappy with her choice of husband, whom he described as "rather dull."[2] He felt Sharon could have married anyone she wanted and, at 21, had not waited long enough to find a more suitable groom.

Perhaps Disney was more concerned about becoming lonely than being disappointed with the man Sharon had chosen to marry. The 58-year-old Disney became depressed at how empty the house in which he and Lillian lived seemed to be without their children.

His enterprises had become so large that he felt less a part of them as time went on. Disney no longer

Grandchildren

When Disney's daughter Diane announced that she was pregnant for the first time, Disney dearly hoped that she would name her son after him. Instead, Diane and Ron named their new son Christopher. Walt was deeply disappointed. Diane and Ron had three girls before having another son, whom they named Walter Elias Disney Miller.

Disney spends time with his family at Disneyland.

produced cartoon shorts, opting instead for full-
length animated and live-action movies. Among
these was the live-action film *Old Yeller*. Released

in 1957, it earned more than $10 million. The animated *Sleeping Beauty* earned $5.3 million in 1959, but it was his most expensive film to make and proved to be a financial disappointment.

Disney also produced a series of family comedies in the late 1950s and early 1960s. These included *The Shaggy Dog*, a 1959 film about a teenager who is transformed into a dog, and *The Absent-Minded Professor*, a 1961 movie about a scientist who discovers a substance called "flubber" that can make cars fly. *The Absent-Minded Professor* did so well that Disney decided to produce a sequel, something he usually avoided. The sequel, *Son of Flubber*, did very well at the box office. Sources differ, but estimates show that by 1960, Walt Disney Productions was worth between $60 and $80 million, making it one of the wealthiest movie studios in the world.

The Acting Bug

The entertainment bug bit Disney's second daughter, but not for long. Soon after returning from a school in Switzerland, Sharon Disney decided she wanted to become an actress. Her father provided a small role for her in the Disney movie, *Johnny Tremain*, which was a film adaptation of a book about the Revolutionary War. Sharon, however, quickly lost her interest in acting. She married soon thereafter.

A STUDIO CHANGE

In the late 1950s, Disney had changed the name of his *Disneyland* show to *Walt Disney Presents*. He still remained the host of the show, and would continue to host the show until his death. But in 1961, a disagreement with ABC prompted Disney to move *Walt Disney Presents* to NBC and rename it *Walt Disney's Wonderful World of Color*. The show was broadcast in color, and remained a Sunday night staple on that network for two decades.

Disney built a new home in the desert near Palm Springs, California. Lillian, however, was so attached to the house in which their kids were raised that she rarely visited the new home. Her husband spent much of his time golfing or bowling, which had become his new athletic passions. He also spent time building miniatures out of wood.

Great Honors

Disney's influence on American culture impressed even those at the top. Among those who praised him for his work with kids was President Dwight Eisenhower, who sent a telegram that was presented at a 1957 banquet honoring Disney. It read: "Your genius as a creator of folklore has long been recognized by leaders in every field of human endeavor, including . . . the children of this land and all lands."[3]

Eyes to the Future

By the early 1960s, Disney became concerned about his health and began thinking about who would take over his duties at the studio. His choice was his son-in-law Ron Miller, Diane's husband. Miller had ended his one-year professional football career, during which he was knocked unconscious in a game. Miller wanted to learn as much as he could from his father-in-law about the movie business. Disney soon made Miller the director of the television segments on *Walt Disney's Wonderful World of Color*.

Miller did not receive high grades from many staff members. Neither did Roy's son Roy E., who also rose to prominence at the studio. But Disney was becoming increasingly interested in enjoying his personal life. Disney spent a lot of time with his family, and he particularly enjoyed playing with his grandchildren. He and Lillian traveled to Europe in 1961, not only for enjoyment but also to tour the new amusement parks that had been built throughout the continent. He hoped to gain ideas to improve Disneyland.

Disney, however, was growing increasingly tired and achy. He had not taken care of himself

particularly well over the years. He had slept too little and smoked too much. He had chronic pain from an old sports injury. There would be more professional successes and personal joys in Disney's life. But that life would be tragically cut short soon. ⌐

*Ron Miller, left, and Roy E. Disney, right,
were both employed by Walt Disney.*

Hayley Mills appeared in The Parent Trap *in 1961.*

TRIUMPH AND TRAGEDY

alt Disney was not particularly old, but he felt old in the early 1960s. His body ached from overwork, and he began to think about his own mortality. Disney set priorities for the remainder of his life. If he was close to the end, he wanted to go out with a bang. And that is what he did. The Disney studio created memorable live-action and animated films as his health deteriorated. Live-action movies such as *Swiss Family Robinson* and *Pollyanna*, which featured Hayley Mills, fared quite well. The success of *Old Yeller* in 1957 motivated Disney to produce more movies about animals. The result was the animated *101 Dalmatians*, released in 1961, which performed very well at the box office.

But no Disney production of the early 1960s matched the success of *Mary Poppins*. Disney put all his energies into what became a sensation throughout the country and one of the most beloved movies ever made. The combination live-action and animated musical about a magical nanny featured Julie Andrews, who had made her name in Broadway plays, and television star Dick Van Dyke.

British Star

One of the most popular actresses to appear in Disney movies was Hayley Mills. The pretty, blond British actress made six Disney films starting when she was 12 years old. Disney was so taken with Mills that he ordered the posh Beverly Hills hotel room in which she and her family were staying to be filled with flowers, fruits, and candy. He also gave them all a personal tour of Disneyland.

The main character, Mary Poppins, gave affection to the children of a rich father who paid little attention to them. She also charmed audiences with her humor and singing. Songs such as "Chim Chim Cheree," "Supercalifragilisticexpialidocious," and "Just a Spoonful of Sugar" delighted movie patrons, young and old.

Folks streamed to the theaters to see *Mary Poppins*. It earned more than $44 million and was recognized as one of Disney's most brilliant productions. It earned an incredible 13 Academy Award nominations and won five Oscars, including one for Special Visual

A Daughter's Idea

Walt Disney might never have turned *Mary Poppins* into one of the greatest musicals of all time if not for the prodding of daughter Diane. *Mary Poppins* was a series of books written by novelist P. L. Travers. The first was published in 1934. Disney considered it a fine tale for children, and Lillian often read it to Diane at night if she was struggling to fall asleep. The child was so taken by the book that she often asked her father if he could take it to the silver screen. Even Lillian believed it would make a wonderful film.

Disney first approached Travers during World War II to ask permission to make a movie out of her book. Travers was born in Australia, but spent most of her adult life in London, England, from which she moved to avoid the bombing during the war. Travers turned him down flat, just as she had done to representatives of other movie studios.

In 1960, the persistent Disney traveled to meet Travers in England, to which she had returned. When he promised he would not turn her novel into a cartoon, the elderly author gave her consent to allow him to go forward with the film.

Effects. Andrews earned another for Best Actress.

Disney had been showered with compliments through much of his career, but the praise reached its highest level after the release of *Mary Poppins*. In 1964, President Lyndon Johnson presented him with the Presidential Medal of Freedom, the highest honor that can be earned by a civilian.

Van Dyke

Dick Van Dyke, one of the stars of *Mary Poppins*, was still working as the lead actor in an extremely popular television show while he was making the film. *The Dick Van Dyke Show* was about a comedy writer living with his wife and young son in New York. The show won 15 Emmy Awards during its five seasons on the air.

Second Theme Park Dream

Disney did not rest on his laurels. He was soon talking with those who built Disneyland about creating another theme park in Florida. He envisioned not just an amusement park, but also a world of tomorrow that would give visitors a glimpse of what the future might look like.

The perfect showcase was on the horizon. Disney worked on several attractions for the 1964 World's Fair in New York City. Among his projects was Great Moments with Mr. Lincoln, which featured a mechanically controlled, life-sized robot of the sixteenth president of the United States.

An early model of EPCOT, created in 1961

Soon Disney spent $5 million for 43 square miles (11,137 ha) of swampland near Orlando, Florida. It represented an area about 150 times greater than that of Disneyland. The purchase was kept a secret because if people learned that a new Disney theme park was being planned, the price of the land would have skyrocketed.

The public did not remain in the dark, however. The plan leaked out in early 1965, which increased the cost of each acre from $200 to $1,000. However, Disney's purchase had been completed before land prices increased.

Disney was particularly passionate about what became known as the City of Tomorrow. This was the most ambitious project in the proposed new park. It would eventually be called EPCOT—the Experimental Prototype Community of Tomorrow.

The Last Days

But the man who created EPCOT would not live to see it. Nor would he enjoy the opening of the entire theme park, which would be called Walt Disney World. By early 1966, Disney's health was rapidly declining. His neck and back gave him greater discomfort than ever. Doctors informed him that only an operation could relieve the pain.

Disney wasted no time getting to the root of his illness. He was stunned to learn that X-rays showed a dark mass about the size of a walnut in his left lung. His heavy smoking habit had resulted in lung cancer. He underwent surgery less than a week later and learned that his condition was worse than first anticipated. Doctors gave him the distressing news

Life Expectancy

Disney would have been shocked had he been told in the early 1950s that he would live just another decade. He believed that anyone in his family was destined for a long life. When his uncle Robert turned 85 years old in 1951, Disney wrote that longevity seemed to run on both sides of the family. A month later he wrote that his current health and the long life spans of his ancestors all foretold a long life for him.

that his cancer was in its advanced stages, which caused the removal of his entire lung. But the cancer had spread beyond his lungs. Soon the doctors were informing Lillian and his two daughters that Disney had between six months and two years to live.

By late November, Disney's pain increased. He could no longer work other than watching over others. He entered the hospital on November 30 and was visited often by Lillian, Diane, Sharon, and Roy.

Disney knew it was over. And at midnight on December 15, 1966, he asked that the head of his bed be raised so he could gaze out the window at his beloved studio one last time. At 9:35 a.m., he died at age 65. The family wanted to grieve in private, so they kept his death a secret for one day. But the world would soon be mourning the loss of a creative genius.

Goodbye

Marc Davis, a veteran animator, knew Disney was dying without having been told. Davis, who had worked with Disney since the 1930s, recalled meeting with him a few weeks before he died. Davis described what he saw after Disney left the room.

"I stayed at the door, and watched him walk down the hall," Davis said. "He was, I guess, about 50 feet away. He turned and said, 'Goodbye, Marc.' He never said goodbye. It was always 'see ya later.'"[1]

Walt Disney on December 23, 1965

Walt Disney and his company have won hundreds of awards for their work.

HONORING A LEGEND

nyone who had been touched by Walt Disney's genius at a movie theater or on television was saddened by his death. But the grief was overwhelming to those closest to him. Among those overcome by sorrow was Roy, who had worked and played side-by-side with his brother for more than half of a century. It was a loss he could barely comprehend.

"I remember standing in the hospital hallway right after Walt died," recalled Patty Disney, Roy's daughter-in-law, "and my father-in-law was consumed with grief. I'd never seen him cry before that. I put my arm around him and he walked away. He wanted to be alone."[1]

There were those who believed that Walt Disney had been taken away from the world before his time. After all, he had not even reached his sixty-sixth birthday, and he certainly planned to witness the opening of Walt Disney World, his new pet project.

Yet many people felt he had provided them with entertainment for five lifetimes. Upon his death, tributes to Disney could be seen or heard in newspapers, news magazines, and television news programs around the world.

A Well-recognized Man

By the time of his death, Walt Disney was among the most awarded people in the entertainment world. Disney won the Presidential Medal of Freedom and the French Legion of Honor. According to the Walt Disney Family Museum, Disney and his animation studio have received 48 Academy Awards, making more than 950 citations or awards total.

Honoring Walt

Perhaps the most touching eulogy was uttered by *CBC Evening News* broadcaster Eric Sevareid, who saw Disney's work as a ray of sunshine in a century torn by war and misery. Sevareid told his viewers,

> *He was an original. Not just an American original, but an original. Period. He was a happy accident, one of the happiest this century has experienced. And judging by the way [the century has been] behaving, in spite of all Disney tried to tell it about laughter, love, children, puppies, and sunrises, the century hardly deserved him. He probably did more to heal—or at least soothe—troubled human spirits than all the psychiatrists in the world.* [2]

On December 16, the day after Disney died, a private funeral was held for family members. Soon thereafter, Roy issued a statement for the studio not only about the loss of

Alive in Spirit

Those who work at Disneyland, Walt Disney World, and Walt Disney Productions still talk about Walt Disney as if he were alive. And in a way he is—in spirit. Among those who expressed that sentiment was Lorraine Santoli, who served as the supervisor of publicity for Disneyland. Though she never met Disney, Santoli said, "His spirit is really alive and all of us who work here feel that. . . . You have a sense that Walt might be peeking around the corner." [3]

his brother, but also about his legacy. Roy was not about to let Walt's dreams die with him:

The death of Walt Disney is a loss to all the people of the world. . . . There is no way to replace Walt Disney. He was an extraordinary man. Perhaps there will never be another like him. (But) we will continue to operate Walt's company in the way that he had established and guided it. All of the plans for the future that Walt had begun will continue to move ahead.[4]

Some were not so sure. Original Disneyland designer Marvin Davis, who was planning to work on Walt Disney

Mourning All Over

The death of Walt Disney touched not only Americans. People from all over the world were grieving. Condolences were sent to the studio from leaders of 12 different countries. Movie stars from various parts of the world also expressed their grief. Included among those was Julie Andrews, who played the title role in the immensely popular *Mary Poppins*, the last highly successful movie Disney produced during his lifetime. Andrews said from England that she was saddened by Disney's passing.

The foreign country in which Disney was most revered was France. In France, Disney was believed to be one of the world's greatest filmmakers. Famed French actor Maurice Chevalier was seen on French television with tears running down his cheeks and expressing his belief that Disney's death was "a disaster for the whole movie world."[5]

A Disney theme park in the capital of France called Disneyland Resort Paris was opened in 1992 and has gained popularity over the years. The park is located in the eastern suburbs of Paris. A second theme park called Walt Disney Studios Park opened in the same area in 2002.

Walt Disney World under construction in 1971

World as well, thought the project might be dead. Roy, however, ended that fear very quickly.

Davis remembered,

> When (Walt) died, we all said, "There goes Disney World." . . . Then, Roy called a meeting in the main studio projection room. And all the main people who were involved in Disney World were there. I've never heard a more profoundly brave, gutsy speech in my life. (Roy) had just buried his brother, and he was giving us all a pep talk.

He said, "Walt would want us to face this opportunity and by God, we're going to do it!"

When we walked out of there, everybody shook hands and said, "Well, we're going to finish it."[6]

DREAM COME TRUE

In October 1971, the dream indeed came true as Walt Disney World opened in Florida. Just two months after Walt Disney World became a reality, Roy passed away.

Walt Disney continued to inspire those at Walt Disney Productions long after he died. It took a while for the company to catch up with changing tastes, but it finally did in 1987 with the release of *Who Framed Roger Rabbit?* The movie featured a combination of live-action film with animation and was a big hit.

Other classics were to follow. *The Lion King* still ranks as one of the top-selling videocassettes of all time. Other animated films such as *The Little Mermaid*, *Beauty and the Beast*, and *Aladdin* all fared well in the theater and in videocassette and DVD sales.

In Walt's Honor

The original name of the new theme park in Florida was to be Disney World, but Roy had it changed to Walt Disney World to better honor his brother. Roy insisted on the alteration because he believed it would let everyone know that making the park a reality was a dream come true for Walt.

Updated Look

The success of the film *Who Framed Roger Rabbit?* was a direct result of a shakeup at the top of Walt Disney Productions. In 1984, the board of directors named Michael Eisner and Frank Wells to head the studios. They, in turn, lured Jeffrey Katzenberg away from Paramount Pictures. The trio soon worked to give Disney movies an updated look.

The first animated film released after the three newcomers took over was *The Great Mouse Detective*, which performed fairly well at the box office. The highly successful *Who Framed Roger Rabbit?* followed.

But in the end, Disney will be remembered most for the little black mouse he created when animation was still in its infancy. Five years before he died, he was asked why Mickey Mouse had become such a sensation. He replied,

> *Sometimes I've tried to figure out why Mickey appealed to the whole world. Everybody's tried to figure it out. So far as I know, nobody has. He's a pretty nice fellow who never does anybody any harm, who gets into scrapes through no fault of his own, but always manages to come out grinning. . . . Mickey is so simple and uncomplicated, so easy to understand that you can't help liking him.*[7]

Walt Disney was not always as well liked as Mickey. But through his characters, movies, television programs, and theme parks, the impact he made on American society is still visible today. And his genius will live on.

Walt Disney has given the world many memorable characters through his tireless imagination.

TIMELINE

1901

Walter Elias Disney is born in Chicago on December 5.

1915

Disney attends the Kansas City Art Institute.

1917

Disney begins taking night courses at the Chicago Institute of Art in September.

1928

Disney's first silent film featuring Mickey Mouse, titled *Plane Crazy*, premieres at a Los Angeles theater in May.

1928

The Mickey Mouse film *Steamboat Willie* opens on November 18.

1929

The *Silly Symphony* film *The Skeleton Dance* premieres at a Hollywood theater on December 31.

1918

Disney enlists in the American Ambulance Corps, part of the Red Cross.

1919

Disney and Ub Iwerks form Iwerks-Disney Commercial Artists.

1928

Disney and Iwerks modify Oswald the Lucky Rabbit into the first Mickey Mouse character in March.

1930

Columbia Pictures starts advancing Disney $7,000 per cartoon in February.

1934

The Disney animated short *The Three Little Pigs* wins an Academy Award on March 16.

1937

The first full-length animated film, Disney's *Snow White and the Seven Dwarfs*, premieres on December 21.

TIMELINE

1941

Nearly 300 Disney animators go on strike on May 29. The strike ends in September.

1952

Disney forms Walt Disney Incorporated to develop ideas for a theme park that would become Disneyland.

1954

Disney and ABC reach an agreement in April in regard to the creation of Disneyland.

1964

The live-action and animated film *Mary Poppins* premieres in Hollywood on August 27.

1965

Mary Poppins earns several Oscars, including a Best Actress award for Julie Andrews.

1965

Walt and Roy Disney announce plans to build a theme park in Florida.

1954	1955	1955
The *Disneyland* television show debuts on October 27 to an estimated 31 million viewers.	Disneyland opens on July 17.	On October 3, *The Mickey Mouse Club* airs. It features cartoons and the Mouseketeers.

1966	1966	1971
X-rays reveal a cancerous spot on Disney's left lung on November 2.	Disney dies of lung cancer at age 65 on December 15.	Walt Disney World opens on October 25. Roy Disney dedicates the park to his brother.

Essential Facts

Date of Birth

December 5, 1901

Place of Birth

Chicago, Illinois

Date of Death

December 15, 1966

Parents

Elias and Flora Disney

Education

Disney left high school at age 16. He later took classes at the Kansas City Art Institute and the Chicago Institute of Art.

Marriage

Lillian Bounds, July 13, 1925

Children

Diane (biological) and Sharon (adopted)

Career Highlights

Walt Disney's animated pictures include *Steamboat Willie*, *Snow White and the Seven Dwarfs*, and *Peter Pan*. He also produced successful live-action films, including *Mary Poppins*. Disney created popular television shows, such as *The Mickey Mouse Club* and *Walt Disney Presents*. Disney oversaw the creation of Disneyland in California and began work on Walt Disney World in Florida before his death.

Societal Contribution

Walt Disney partnered with charitable organizations, including the Boys and Girls Clubs of America. Disney also gave financial support to St. Joseph's Hospital, and some of his animators helped decorate the children's wing.

Conflicts

❖ Disney's Laugh-O-Grams business went bankrupt in 1923.

❖ In 1926, Disney lost his contract to continue producing the *Alice's Wonderland* cartoons.

❖ In 1930, Ub Iwerks and Carl Stallings left Disney's studio.

Quote

"Sometimes I've tried to figure out why Mickey appealed to the whole world. Everybody's tried to figure it out. So far as I know, nobody has. He's a pretty nice fellow who never does anybody any harm, who gets into scrapes through no fault of his own, but always manages to come out grinning. . . . Mickey is so simple and uncomplicated, so easy to understand that you can't help liking him."—*Walt Disney*

Additional Resources

Select Bibliography

Gabler, Neal. *Walt Disney: The Triumph of the American Imagination*. New York: Alfred A. Knopf, 2006.

Greene, Katherine, and Richard Greene. *The Man Behind the Magic: The Story of Walt Disney*. New York: Penguin Books, 1991.

Mosley, Leonard. *Disney's World*. Lanham, MD: Scarborough House, 1990.

Thomas, Bob. *Walt Disney: An American Original*. New York: Hyperion, 1994.

Further Reading

Barrier, Michael. *The Animated Man: A Life of Walt Disney*. Berkeley, CA: University of California Press, 2008.

Canemaker, John. *Walt Disney's Nine Old Men and the Art of Animation*. New York: Disney Press, 2001.

Fanning, Jim. *Walt Disney*. New York: Chelsea House, 1994.

Green, Howard E. *Remembering Walt*. New York: Disney Editions, 2002.

Hammontree, Marie. *Walt Disney: Young Movie Maker*. New York: Simon & Schuster, 1997.

Tieman, Robert. *The Mickey Mouse Treasures*. New York: Disney Editions, 2007.

Watts, Steven. *The Magic Kingdom: Walt Disney and the American Way of Life*. Columbia, MO: University of Missouri Press, 2001.

Web Links

To learn more about Walt Disney, visit ABDO Publishing Company online at **www.abdopublishing.com**. Web sites about Walt Disney are featured on our Book Links page. These links are routinely monitored and updated to provide the most current information available.

Places to Visit

Disneyland Resort
1313 Harbor Boulevard, Anaheim, CA 92802
714-520-5060
disneyland.disney.go.com
The first Disney theme park features several attractions, including Main Street, USA; Adventureland; Tomorrowland; Fantasyland; and Frontierland.

Walt Disney Hometown Museum
120 East Santa Fe Street, Marceline, MO 64658
660-376-3343
www.waltdisneymuseum.org
This museum is located in Walt Disney's hometown of Marceline, Missouri. Exhibits, letters, and artifacts tell the story of Disney's home life and young years.

Walt Disney World Resort
Lake Buena Vista, FL 32830
407-560-7959
disneyworld.disney.go.com
This huge park near Orlando, Florida, features four theme parks and two water parks. Among those are Magic Kingdom, Epcot Center, Disney's Hollywood Studios, and Disney's Animal Kingdom.

GLOSSARY

Academy Awards
An annual event honoring the best in movies during the previous year.

accompany
To play live music to complement a silent movie.

animation
The entire process of preparing animated cartoons.

aptitude
An ability for something.

armistice
An agreement or truce between warring nations.

contract
An agreement written and signed by two or more people or businesses for the purpose of completing a specified task.

copyright
The exclusive right to a literary, musical, or artistic work, generally for the purpose of making money.

director
One who directs the action of a play or movie.

distributor
A person or company engaged in the general marketing and selling of goods or services.

Great Depression
The era from the end of 1929 until the early 1940s of extreme economic hardship in the United States.

immaculate
Clean, spotless.

merchandise
Any tangible item for sale.

mortality
The state of being subject to death.

motion picture
> A movie or film.

novelties
> An item used for decoration or amusement.

omen
> A sign of things to come.

Oscar
> The statue earned by those who win an Academy Award.

picket line
> A line of people who are on strike or protesting.

primitive
> Basic or undeveloped.

production
> The entire process of making a television show, movie, or play.

sketch
> A simple drawing or painting, usually done before adding details.

strike
> To engage in a work stoppage with the goal of receiving higher pay or better working conditions.

studio
> The workroom of anyone in an artistic field.

sultry
> Hot and humid.

tetanus
> An infectious disease caused by a specific bacteria, often through a wound.

tuberculosis
> A bacterial disease that affects the lungs.

union
> An organized group of workers united for a common purpose.

Source Notes

Chapter 1. Making of a Mouse
1. Neal Gabler. *Walt Disney: The Triumph of the American Imagination*. New York: Alfred A. Knopf, 2006. 111.

Chapter 2. Walt's Wild Imagination
1. Katherine Greene and Richard Greene. *The Man Behind the Magic: The Story of Walt Disney*. New York: Penguin Books, 1991. 8.

Chapter 3. Missed War, New Career
1. Neal Gabler. *Walt Disney: The Triumph of the American Imagination*. New York: Alfred A. Knopf, 2006. 40.

Chapter 4. Go West, Young Man
1. Neal Gabler. *Walt Disney: The Triumph of the American Imagination*. New York: Alfred A. Knopf, 2006. 47.
2. Leonard Mosley. *Disney's World*. Lanham, MD: Scarborough House, 1990. 76–77.

Chapter 5. Depressed in the Depression
1. Neal Gabler. *Walt Disney: The Triumph of the American Imagination*. New York: Alfred A. Knopf, 2006. 134.
2. Marc Eliot. *Walt Disney: Hollywood's Dark Prince*. New York: Carol Publishing Group, 1993. 58.

Chapter 6. Seven Dwarfs and One Strike
1. "Franklin D. Roosevelt." *The White House*. 22 Sept. 2008 <http://www.whitehouse.gov/history/presidents/fr32.html>.
2. Marc Eliot. *Walt Disney: Hollywood's Dark Prince*. New York: Carol Publishing Group, 1993. 101–102.

Chapter 7. Television and a Fantasy Land
1. "The Family Grows." *The Walt Disney Family Museum*. 15 Dec. 2008 <http://disney.go.com/disneyatoz/familymuseum/collection/biography/familygrows/index.html>.
2. Katherine Greene and Richard Greene. *The Man Behind the Magic: The Story of Walt Disney*. New York: Penguin Books, 1991. 116.

Chapter 8. "M-I-C-K-E-Y M-O-U-S-E!"
1. "Mickey Mouse Club." *FiftiesWeb.com*. 8 Oct. 2008 <http://www.fiftiesweb.com/annette.htm>.
2. Marc Eliot. *Walt Disney: Hollywood's Dark Prince*. New York: Carol Publishing Group, 1993. 247.
3. Ibid. 245.

Chapter 9. Triumph and Tragedy
1. Katherine Greene and Richard Greene. *The Man Behind the Magic: The Story of Walt Disney*. New York: Penguin Books, 1991. 168.

Source Notes Continued

Chapter 10. Honoring a Legend

1. Katherine Greene and Richard Greene. *The Man Behind the Magic: The Story of Walt Disney*. New York: Penguin Books, 1991. 170.

2. Brian Bennett. "A Tribute to Walter Elias Disney." *Mouse Planet*. 26 Aug. 2008 <http://www.mouseplanet.com/dtp/archive/other/tribute/htm>.

3. Katherine Greene and Richard Greene. *The Man Behind the Magic: The Story of Walt Disney*. New York: Penguin Books, 1991. 173.

4. Neal Gabler. *Walt Disney: The Triumph of the American Imagination*. New York: Alfred A. Knopf, 2006. 631.

5. Marc Eliot. *Walt Disney: Hollywood's Dark Prince*. New York: Carol Publishing Group, 1993. 268.

6. Katherine Greene and Richard Greene. *The Man Behind the Magic: The Story of Walt Disney*. New York: Penguin Books, 1991. 172.

7. "Disney, Walter Elias." Statler Family Obituaries. 8 Oct. 2008 <http://freepages.genealogy.rootsweb.ancestry.com/~statler/statler/obits/disneywalterelias.html>.

INDEX

Absent-Minded Professor, The, 75
Academy Awards, 49, 57,
    82–83, 89
Aladdin, 93
Alice cartoons, 36, 37–39, 43
Alice in Wonderland, 63, 64
Andrews, Julie, 81, 83, 91

Bambi, 58
Beauty and the Beast, 93
betrayal, 8–9, 10, 59
Brown, Bob, 73

Chaplin, Charlie, 21, 30
Cinderella, 35, 64
Cinephone, 14, 45
Cohn, Harry, 46
color animation, 49
color television, 65–66
copyrights, 8

Davy Crockett, 67, 71
"Disney's Folly," 56
Disney products, 72
Disney, Diane (daughter), 50,
    52, 63, 64, 73, 77, 82, 86
Disney, Elias (father), 16–17,
    18, 19–20, 21, 22, 25,
    26–27, 35, 57–58
Disney, Flora (Call) (mother),
    17, 19, 25, 27, 35, 57, 58
Disney, Herbert (brother), 17,
    18, 21, 26, 27, 35
Disney, Lillian (Bounds) (wife),
    7, 9, 40, 46, 48, 50, 56, 65,
    67, 73, 76, 77, 82, 86

Disney, Raymond (brother), 17,
    18, 21, 25
Disney, Roy (brother)
    business with Walt Disney, 11,
        27, 37, 38–39, 42, 49,
        59, 64, 67
    childhood, 17, 19, 20
    children, 46, 77
    death of Walt Disney, 86
    marriage, 40
    tuberculosis, 35, 37, 38
    World War I, 24–25, 26
Disney, Roy E. (nephew), 46,
    77
Disney, Ruth (sister), 17, 19, 35
Disney, Sharon (daughter), 56,
    58, 63, 73, 75, 86
Disney, Walt
    childhood, 17–22
    death, 86
    depression, 27–29, 47–49,
        50, 73
    education, 20–22
    International Red Cross,
        25–26
    lung cancer, 85–86
Disneyland (television show),
    65, 66–67, 71, 76
Disneyland (theme park), 65,
    67–68, 71, 72, 77, 81, 83,
    84, 90, 91

Experimental Prototype
    Community of Tomorrow, 85

Index Continued

fairy tales, 19, 35, 54, 57
Fantasia, 58
Felix the Cat, 30, 43, 44
Freleng, Friz, 8
French Legion of Honor, 89
full-length animated features, 54–57, 58, 74

goodwill tour, 59
Great Depression, 44, 45, 53, 56, 63

Iwerks, Ub, 8, 9, 10, 13, 28–31, 35, 36, 39, 45, 46
Iwerks-Disney Commercial Artists, 29

Jazz Singer, The, 13

Kansas City Film Ad Company, 30, 31–32, 34, 35, 36, 39
Kansas City Star, 27, 30

Lady and the Tramp, 71
Laemmle, Carl, 7, 43
Laugh-O-Grams, 31–32, 34–36
Lion King, The, 93
Little Mermaid, The, 93

Marceline, Missouri, 17
Mary Poppins, 81–83, 91
MGM, 36
Mickey Mouse
    creation of, 9–14, 40, 44
    Gallopin' Gaucho, The, 11, 13
    Plane Crazy, 9, 10, 12

popularity, 45, 49, 58, 72, 94
    Steamboat Willie, 13, 14
Mickey Mouse Club, The, 71, 72
military training films, 63
Miller, Ron, 64, 73, 77
Mills, Hayley, 81
Minnie Mouse, 44
Mintz, Charles, 7–8, 9, 10, 43–44
Mouseketeers, 71

Old Yeller, 74, 81
101 Dalmatians, 81
Orlando, Florida, 84
Oswald the Lucky Rabbit
    Poor Papa, 7
    Walt Disney and, 6–8, 10, 43–44

Pearl Harbor, 60, 62
Pesmen-Rubin Studios, 27–28
Peter Pan, 63, 64
Pfeiffer, Walter, 21, 29
Pinocchio, 58
Pollyanna, 81
Powers, Pat, 14, 45–46
Presidential Medal of Freedom, 83, 89

Reichenbach, Harry, 14

Sevareid, Eric, 90
Shaggy Dog, The, 75
silent movies, 13, 21, 30, 36, 37
Silly Symphonies
   creation of, 44
   Flowers and Trees, 49
   Golden Touch, The, 57
   Skeleton Dance, The, 44–45
   success, 49, 58
Sleeping Beauty, 75
Snow White and the Seven Dwarfs,
   54–57, 58, 64
So Dear to My Heart, 63
Son of Flubber, 75
Song of the South, 63
sound animation, 11–14, 44
strikes, 58–59
Swiss Family Robinson, 81

talkies, 13, 49
technology, 13, 31
Three Little Pigs, The, 19, 49, 53, 57
Treasure Island, 64
True-Life Adventures, 64
tuberculosis, 35, 37
20,000 Leagues Under the Sea, 71
typhoid fever, 21

Universal Pictures, 6–7, 8, 9,
   43, 44

Van Dyke, Dick, 81, 83

Walt Disney Presents, 76
Walt Disney World, 83–85, 89,
   90, 91–93
Walt Disney's Wonderful World of Color,
   76, 77
Warner Bros., 8, 13, 36
Who Framed Roger Rabbit?, 93, 94
Winkler, George, 7
Winkler, Margaret, 37–38, 39,
   43
World War I, 22, 24–25, 26
World War II, 60, 62–63, 82
World's Fair, 83

Zorro, 71–72

About the Author

Martin Gitlin is a freelance writer based in Cleveland, Ohio. He has written more than a dozen educational books. These include biographies about NASCAR drivers Jimmie Johnson and Jeff Gordon and historical books about the Battle of the Little Bighorn, the stock market crash, and the landmark *Brown v. Board of Education* Supreme Court decision. Gitlin has won more than 45 awards during his 25 years as a writer, including first place for general excellence from Associated Press. He lives with his wife and three children.

Photo Credits

Hulton Archives/Stringer/Getty Images, cover; Itsuo Inouye/AP Images, 6; Michael Ochs Archives/Stringer/Getty Images, 12; Getty Images, 15, 41; Bettmann/Corbis, 16, 28; AP Images, 23, 24, 33, 42, 47, 51, 52, 55, 62, 66, 79, 87, 92; Topical Press Agency/Stringer/Getty Images, 34; Popperfoto/Getty Images, 61; Asher Welstead/iStock Photo, 69; Peter Stackpole/Time Life Pictures/Getty Images, 70; Gene Lester/Getty Images, 74; Silver Screen Collection/Hulton Archive/Getty Images, 80; Keystone/CNP/Getty Images, 84; Dick Strobel/AP Images, 88; Alfred Eisenstaedt//Time Life Pictures/Getty Images, 95